Cruel Roses

Cruel Roses

Poems by

Judith Ann Levison

Kelsay Books

Cover art: Judith Ann Levison

Cover design: Shay Culligan

ISBN: 978-1-949229-10-3

Kelsay Books
Aldrich Press
www.kelsaybooks.com

For
Peter Green
Maria and Al Holt
Ruth Merritt

Acknowledgments

Albatross: "A Maine Childhood," "Winter Evening"
Kent State University: "Lessons," "Record Player," "Sunshine"
Pennine UK: "Trust Betrayed"
The Alembic: "Eclipse"
Willow Review: "Early Development," "Reform School," "Love Lock," "At the Exhibition"
Edgz: "A Child's Epiphany"
Evansville Review: "Red Riding Hood," "Deer Head"
The Soul's Bright Home: "Grandson," "Lincoln Memorial"
Paterson Literary: "Shoes"
Buffalo Carp: "White Barrette"
Literary Town Hall: "Cleopatra"
Scars Publication: "Red Mittens"
Cold Mountain Review: "Betrayal"
Free Verse: "Sand Cradle," "Two Men on a Bench in a Great City"
Ship of Fools: "A Woman Remembered," "Her Way with It," "Through the Oval"
Shadows & Light: "A Spell"
Ibbetson Street Press: "Small Chapters"
Open Minds Quarterly: "Marry Me," "Canvas," "Yellow Corsage," "Emily Rose," "Meditation," "The Hesper and the Luther Little"
The Electric Muse: "Ana and the Painting," "Abstract Love," "Indian Luck"
Studio One: "Masterpiece Theater"
Chryslas Transaction: "Fair Love"
Plainspoke: "Near Love"
Common Ground Review: "Prize"
The Poet's Pen: "Moon Phobia," "The Gas Station"
Plainsongs: "Vietnam Sun"
Literary Town Hall Anthology: "Guardianship"
Pennsylvania Magazine: "The Scarecrow"
Pegasus: "English 101," "Promise"

The New Yorker: "Mary Shellmic"
Poets' Espresso Review: "Sleeping Beauty"
Stray Branch: "Editorial"
The Sheltered Poet: "Lemonade"
Story Teller: "Poor Reader"
The Talking River: "Graduation Dance"
The Hollins Critic: "Attachment"
California Quarterly: "Kingdom Come," "Pill Box Hat"
Earthshine: "The Black Empire"
Princeton Spectrum: "Marriage Duel," "The Women by the Creek"
Common Ground Review: "Pirate Ship Ring," "Beautiful Fur
    Coats"
Soul Fountain: "Name"
Poetalk: "Oak Leaves"
Yasquezine: "Mt. Katahdin"
Mudfish: "Lineage"
Delhousie Review: "Cross above the Stove"
Where Our Voices Fly: "Old Gloves"
First Class: "Apple Pie"
Dal Review: "Brownie Camera"
Timber Creek Review: "Red Sandals"
Feelings of the Heart: "Crosswords"
Shemom: "Symbols," "Out of the Country"
Portland Review: "Harp," "Languages"
Northern Stars: "Deliverance"
Blue Unicorn: "Scar"
Orbis: "Getting Out"
Painted Bride Quarterly: "Slipping through a Life"
Haight Asbury Literary Journal: "Work Horses"
Cold Mountain Review: "Cigar"
Homestead Review: "Star Fish"
Caveat Lector: "Sorrow"
Agni: "Duties"
Lonestar: "A Little Life"
Iconoclast: "Last Act"

Contents

Deer Head

Through the Oval

Trust Betrayed

A Maine Childhood

I often dream of the wretched
place I called home.
As I age memories lose their protective glow.
Stark, beautiful trees felled in wild succession
Are determined by the wind and skill of the cutter.

I know the outhouse still stands far from the house,
a journey toward the hell of poverty's grim hold.
I ploughed through knee deep snow with bare legs.
The dark was timed as if from a clock inside the moon.

Sapphires glinted over small hills in a pale blue glow,
pushing me forward to the crooked door shut with snow,
a red shovel beside it.

Lessons

They are as near me in death
as they were distant to me in life.

Forgiveness disarms me and I want to
run from the shack for cover in the woods.

Neither of my parents had mothers,
ignorant of love they tortured us.

Nightmares have double mirrors,
I forgive, I forgive not.
Daises do not have petals enough
for a childhood rooted in a mother and
father hardened and indifferent.

Bravery it was to listen to the harsh
words of my parents, speaking from
Vodka's clinking dirge.
Sleepwalking, I rose from my bed and
stared at them without seeing.

I longed for school, a sturdy desk, my pencils
and books in order. The principal's heels
clicking with confidence on the gray tiles.

October, it was raining and ominous,
but I loved the cozy room,
our colorful paper leaves on the window.
I shivered in a thin sweater wishing
for a raincoat.

My tutor tugged me awake for my reading
lesson. I pretended I could not read well.
She was strict, but sat close to me.

Trust Betrayed

The first day of school my teacher
Had silk roses tied in her braids.
She seemed like a lissome flower.
Was I on Venus or Mars?
Or was this a picture show of Heaven?
Suddenly I knew this was a place
Truth could be spoken,
Not hiding in a closet listening to
My mother's rages, dirty jokes, and
Drawling vowels.

When I rose from my crudely-carved desk
My pearl necklace broke,
Together we gathered the beads,
I'll restring them she said.
Dizzy from kindness, undeserving
I said *I love you,* not thank you.

By the end of the week, I hugged her,
Reassured I had found a real mother.
At home my woes continued: torn hair,
Bruises the color of marbles, casually
She said I'm calling your mother.

Realizing the consequences of her words,
I cried on the bus.
I ran but the switch scratched my legs
Until pencil thin blood marked me.

Next day at school, I would not look at her.
What did she know of trust and feckless love?
Seldom do I rage but on that day
I threw away those pearls
And we were even.

Eclipse

It was noon.
I could not look at the sun's shutting eye.
My world was becoming a black shroud
from this moving lid of death.
My chest swelled in a sphere of panic.
When I opened my eyes, someone yelled
"Don't look!"
Father wore a scary welding mask.
He held a can of beer with a bee on the rim.

I clung to my dolls in a stroller,
threw a blanket over them,
for their eyes were made of glass
and could reflect the dying sun.

Early Development

I move through life with one book after another.
It is a way of forgetting monstrosities, however small or far away.
The collapse of my youth started on an autumn day when I was
four.

When I am with old friends, after an hour or so, my mind
Begins to fade.
Despite these wondrous days of love and communion
In the withering present, I forget their questions.
Weary of the past intruding into the present, I can hardly speak
And keep up conversation. It happens daily.
Excusing myself from life, I lie down and let the tides of cold
Exhaustion sweep over me.
Shaking, I settle emotion down as meditation spins old love songs.

The monstrous act was diminutive; many children of poor,
Drinking families survived worse every sparkling day and nights
The moon coldly watched.
Four. I was fidgeting in a blue and cream square wool coat.
Mother slapped my face and pushed me toward the hideous,
Unruly bus.
Dazed all my first day, I wanted to sleep at my wooden desk.
Disappear Forever.

Record Player

It was true then. My mother would not
Allow the record player in the house.
Her nerves were shot. Get rid of it.
I nearly dropped it taking it to the garage's
Gruesome world of black spiders and
Kerosene cans. I carefully placed it on
The bench amidst the filthy maze of father's tools,
Beneath his gun racks and deer antlers
Twisted like gaping soundless mouths.

For a month I listened to Gene Autrey's
"Buttons and Bows". My world was released
Into a lost landscape where
The windows were so dirty it appeared
To be raining outside.
The musical life of the record player was brief.
I stepped in kerosene and my mother said
I was banned from the garage and the record
Player was taken in my father's truck to the
Burning hills of a dump's wastcland where its
Musical echo still reached me.

Feeling numb I went to the garage the next day.
A fat spider landed on my head and I ran
Screaming, sobbing from the garage,
I pulled it off behind the chicken house.

A year later, on my radio, I heard "Fly Me to the Moon."
I remained there for the duration of my childhood.

A Child's Epiphany

Battered, dresses always torn,
I visited my aunt's house where
Flat blossoms moved on wallpaper.
In her ten-cushion living room there
Was a white cross with a skinny man
Pinned to it in three places, his head
Cast down like a broken flower.
As my aunt wiped 'merciful Jesus' with
A hand towel, cross-stitched in pale green,
The halo from His head passed to mine unseen.
At home, liquor which sent minds far away
And the bitter taste of dandelions deeply
Gouged from the dirt would now remind
Him: I lived far below a child's proper worth.

Later, I sat beneath a cherry tree to watch,
Blossoms flatten upon the stone walk.
Waiting for signs to keep my elation as
High as a lost balloon—not knowing when
It would burst, or if my thirst could again
Drink at a rusty well, far from this
White grandeur, blood tingeing
Each petal stuck to my hair in a halo.

Winter Evening

Winter takes shape as a glistening
helmet over our house. Trees suffer
bandaged with ice. The mail box empty.
Waiting months for his letter, he does not need me.
A shot is heard. Later father is bent
dragging a deer carcass.
Soon we will eat blood cooked into gravy.
Mother sings Hank Snow songs as
she roasts a venison dinner. I gag on meat.
Winter broods in her until she rants like an
animal in a cage, smoking, pacing.
Dead now a decade, I still fear her.
She had a way of breaking my life apart,
Until I received his next letter.

Red Riding Hood

I said my mother was evil
yet, rarely mentioned malignant facts,
for she hated sounds of giggling, urgent whispers
or the brush of my skirt in the woods—could I hear
the wolves she asked?

One day when fiddleheads coiled a bashful green,
I followed behind her, fell into a boarded well,
hanging onto roots, she pulled me out impatiently.
Nails digging into my wrists, furious and gasping,
she dragged me home, had to have a cigarette.
I brought her one and was sent to my room.
It was not painted, but there were knickknacks.
I still have the tea cup and little spoon.

She read bloody mysteries while crocheting
butterflies, snowflakes and daisies. I might have one
put away. Once I said something as I neared her lap,
then a fierce hurl swatted me back like a fly.

They found my mother wandering in the woods
singing old country ballads and looking for wolves.
Later, from a green craft room she wrote loving letters.
We'd have tea and biscuits when she got home.

I now see psychiatrists, but it does no good.
The stories lack believability, no wolves, no hood.

Grandson

When I wish to be happy
I think of my grandson.
He is beautiful with his large
dark eyes, his long body of energy.
Now three, I see highlights of behavior
hopefully replicated in future years.
Aching for him to remember me
as more than an anxious shadow, latent
in our play, leaves a poignant memory
until I see him again.

He has a golden life in a charmed world.
His innocence is as pure as white
Floating Hearts flowers in placid ponds.
I never thought a miracle grandson would be a gift
after my loveless, abusive parents.
May he never know the petals of its secrets,
for only then will that world vanish.

Shoes

All my life I await the balmy mysteries of spring.

Need sufficed when once I could run the fields.
Dew-layered in the morning my cold wet ankles
Were encircled by purple violets that I leaned to
Pick one by one.

I could not bear to tell my mother the new
Oxfords had holes.

The agony and punishment of poverty oppressed me.
I put cardboard in the shoes, I could read
Lessons again while holding my feet up on the swings.

Damned, I scraped them to make sudden stops.
Swinging to me was like flying into the skies'
Enraptured blue where no one could reach me.

Yet hiding them became unbearable. Trembling, I held
Out to my mother taped holes and wet socks brown with mud.

Through many days of rain I had to wear them to
Teach me the careless destruction in their pinched life.

In a month a cruel cold filled my lung.
She was not one to bring steaming soup.
I then came down with walking pneumonia.
Alarmed, she called the doctor,
Called me "dear" but it was too late.
I now wore rubber boots to school and
Even good friends laughed.

Next time I will run away barefoot in the fields
Or lose just one shoe, like Cinderella.

White Barrette

Long ago when I was a young girl
Who saw everything and could say nothing,
I saw an owl quiver despite its rigid neck,
Its body tailored white in snow.

I thought of this, and how dark days
Belonged to those who stayed in one place for life,
Layers of winter never quite melting inside them.

One day walking through blue-limbed woods,
I heard behind me the crunching sound of boots—
Familiar, yet unnamable, I flew out of my body
Above homes with lines of frozen sheets,
I made my mind retreat.

There was no place far enough to go.
I looked for signs of the owl's sighting of me,
But only saw myself alone and subdued,
Hair sprouting leaves with white barrette askew.

Cleopatra

My edge has left me
At a party as a friend of a friend
I look for my ex-wife or anyone
That looks like her
In a dark corner I hear a woodpecker
Ferocious and in his element
I call her, she answers hello in a dull drawl
Did the kids get their cards?
Of course, she says, mail box works
The silence lasts the decade of our marriage
I want to linger in the abysmal loneliness
But she says she needs cash for more clothes
She cannot just reinstate herself out there in rags
I think of a red string dress I will buy her
And jewelry similar to those in Cleopatra's museum
An old army man I can bunk anywhere and fill
My boots with cash, she asks suspiciously
What do I want; the d-i-v-o-r-c-e is over

I can't say you are the only one to know me
I miss your trashy ways and I don't know how
To be a father without your help
My dad was a robot with angry voltage
She said I could come over Thanksgiving
Have coffee and pie as long as I did not have any
Ideas, and bring the stuff she wanted, her foot
Now a size 8 and long boots were in style
My Cleopatra, for the scent of sun in my child's hair
I would bring anything to be camouflaged in your life

Red Mittens

He sighed, drank a shot with a pill,
Knew his dramatic sister was in from Paris
To relate near affairs, all going nowhere.
Always tidying his eclectic apartment,
His mother sent plaid grey scarves
And his father played pool with a vengeance
For he was denied a pension, denied success.

None of this interested him.

Outside the bus window the snow stalled.
It would dissipate or make a show of it.
The man with baggy eyes beside him
Was quite keen on old cars, antiques and
Never went to church—all that death,
Misused authority, and weeping.
On his right a woman declared everyone
Had their own lodestar angel of light
You just had to look for it.

Then he saw a little curly haired girl turning
Her red mittens over and over.
She sniffed the inside of each and bit
The string that bound them.

Her brother then grabbed them, with raw laughter,
Tossed the mittens in the slushy gutter.

Reform School

Terror has made my life poignant.
Generous, tight fields of tulips make roots
of deep and long tunnels while under summer
sheets we whisper.
With everyone drunk, we are afraid to pass
through the kitchen, our lips red from lollypops.
We are getting hungry and thirsty.
It was decided my sister being older, could run faster,
and being boyish, did not get smacked around.
If I went, I would be snagged and they would pretend
to spank me or pack my suitcase for reform school.
I was thrilled to go to school, jumped up and down,
But they laughed and threw my clothes in the stove.

A Woman Remembered

Betrayal

It is the wind talking
Back and forth
I have not said a word

It is the seer of all torn
Leaves and holds my face
Up toward black branches
To see what I must see
Musty colors amidst rose

I hear two voices murmur
And laugh from the nearby barn

For we held hands all our lives
And in the circle meant never
To let go until the last ash of us all
Refused to glow

Husband enters with my friend
The pot whistles as if a train
Will derail
Her red hair held up by butterfly
Pins is loosened

I take their cold hands
And the wind roars
I do not want to hear any more

Sand Cradle

My eighteen year old daughter
Now strolls along the seashore.
The wind blows her light hair back
Into soft wings of gold
That matter only to me.
I sigh, for she thinks of things
I do not know. I must let go
Of my haste to dig a sand cradle,
To be needed again.

During the early evening,
At the entrance of her bedroom door
I practice a blank face.
Candles lit in every corner,
An interlude
Between what was and will be,
Flicker for attention.
I have no courage
Or right to say: *I am here. Listen.*

Before she wiggles into a deep blue dress,
The scent of salt and sun receding,
I go back downstairs to peel
Onions, oranges and rhubarb.
She is not me after all.
Another wave, I gulp,
Rinse the shells off—
The sea's beautiful litter—
Then place them on a shelf.
Dinner alone, I chide myself,
For although I loved hard,
I rarely returned home.

A Woman Remembered

The russet red cabin is far from the crumbling house.
It invites privacy and with one window, suffocation.
The shredded curtain lifts from wind, smoky tinges of rag.
Outside the purplish snake berries bunch in bouquets.
Deer glide by, glare, move in trances. A winter's feast,
But killing is not for today. In his lifetime one woman
With black eyes embraced then exiled him. Deer horns
Hung on the wall talk of dead wanderings. She appears
In the clouds hanging laundry, carrying water,
Staring at him with pity enough to extinguish him. If one
Golden kingdom mattered, it was hers, although her flaws
Would be the fire of his intimate hell. Let it be, hell.

A Spell

A gifted writer, bitter against men,
You did nice things for me,
A prize-winning poetry book signed by the author,
Phone calls listening to my silence, then
Swept away to concerts, museums, I was
Subject to dizziness as if I were in an unreal play
That never would end.

I never told you, out of pride, my life in a shack,
Caring for a toddler, ordered to bed early, I finished
My homework in a cold bath tub lined with a towel.

I would not fathom your interest, a decade older you had
Visions of fireflies where my frailness fit into a jar
You could look at tiny casting lights of manic energy,
My constitution by day stood like broken necks of sunflowers.

Then you left our high school,
I grieved, grasping for air, the sunken cot wet with fever.
My class graduated. My lessons irretrievable, each bookmark
Was a sad measure of my madness.

One day in late June, I opened the window wide
And cold broke the spell.
Womanhood hardened me and after a year you were
Obscured in memory, but not power.

Small Chapters

It was not my choice to have had
brilliant illusory affairs.
Men waved goodbye and left my bedroom
with novels in their breast pockets.
In brief jubilee of these small chapters,
I sipped tea from stained cups.

I remember them all;
on days when wistful, I count
in calculated bliss who gave what—
poetry, a tiny dot scarf, or sagging
dandelion flowers in case I forgot
the county's boring charm,
the tedious scrubbing of the floors,
sunlight on the splinters.

Now I stare at the rain puddles
like scattered hand mirrors
disguising years of mud and grass.
My nightgown folds into the wrinkles
of a roaming ghost.
And when I lie down pain becomes
a blade or hand at my throat.
It is mine or belongs
to someone I wrote.

Marry Me

Throw away that breezy-toned
Letter you scrawl on for lack
Of one true hieroglyphic
And marry me
Why go to a house where
Linen lies thin as paper in drawers
And silver reflects remote eras
As you hear kids squabbling outside
Hoping they never turn out like you
Without a secret kingdom
Where one goes to find this single
Courageous, precious self
Pitted against life's fury

Your hells are small
You dream of ancestors whose
Bold, hawkish names shrivel
You down on a stale pillow

It's now unimaginable to you
We are playing cards on the floor
Interjecting: *honey, sweetie*
My maiden name on luggage by the door
I hint with a stamp of my foot
We must surrender to that kingdom
Where we will find our essence
Wondrous and upside down

Ana and the Painting

With an open palette
The rainbow fuses into
A soft stairway from which
Some can climb to their dreams.

George Seuret paints a Model, Back View, 1887.
Beiges fuse together soft beautiful flesh
In the shape of a contoured vase sitting,
Delicately poised on the edge of the bed,
Her head bent slightly down
As if ashamed, tired, or in pensive meditation,
Her hair piled into a coif from tendrils at her neck.

My wife's back is like polished china
She always turns away from me, as if solemn
In the after images of the day.
Shut out, I compose in my head a short phrase
Using her girlhood name—" Ana dear, I had
A dream last night . . . ."

She pretends to sleep. 1 see the painting
Now as the broken shell of her back.
When I am asleep, the stairway will
Open her dreams and she will remember me.

Masterpiece Theater

I thought it was love
You gave me a satin
Wedding from my flat dream magazine
Later tied the sash at the back
Of my yellow dress
Then bent my head
For an achingly pink strand of pearls
At the dinner table you slowly
Moved my chair in as if I were a child

Such charm was ether
My worries fell like petals at my feet
Picking one up I felt infinite luck
So pure and white with the snap
Of my last hung linen sheet

Now weakened by chemo I looked
Into the glare of my hospital window
I had fuzz on my head like a little old man
The nurses whispered behind masks
I tapped lime Jell-O to test my appetite

I asked you one evening
To bring over my zebra slippers

You said there had been a glitch at work
Tired, *Masterpiece Theater* was on
I knew then I could leave you

Fair Love

Once at a fair years ago,
He could not be sure
If his fingers touched
The cotton of her collar,
Or if the pine aroma from her hair
Wafted through the firefly-studded
Night as the aching began

Now that world revolves
And will not, as in mock ads
At a fair, release him to search for her
Amidst the night's lit cotton candy

Before billboards bleak
With titan muscles, he sees
Caretakers straining to push the wheelchairs
Elated to be out with those like themselves

Seeing her no where, the search spun out
Looking up at the motionless Ferris wheel
He could only hear the paddling
Of the seats and laughter held high

Abstract Love

I have always born a silent message to you.
You choose not to hear it.
My sounds are murmurous.
You know I am waiting as you
Turn to watch the froth and flow of the ocean
And I seek the opposite direction, clusters
Of daisies pronounce their yellow along the road.

We do not tread or break the thin
Thread of our mute liaison.

Listen, I hold a conch to my ear, hear
Whispers: how we became known
Through abstract words, our bodies
Leaning slightly forward, but no kiss possible.

For me you dissolved into bits of heaven,
Now your armor is a pen, writing during
Midnight moods, nonchalant waves of caring.

Near Love

We sat on a cliff above homes with frail chimney smoke.
I do not remember a single word, just a breeze
Curling our hair back from our foreheads.
There was no life before or after us.
It was near love.

I still look out the window to see if he is coming,

In the wheelchair, my mother's body is like a claw.
My sheer will and watchfulness keep her from death
In a ritual of pills, trays and wrinkled bibs,
I am a gracious servant.

One day I push her up to the cliff, old dandelions grow bald
When hit by the chair's wheels. She shrieks with joy
And tries to lift her head when, breathless, we reach the top.

Nothing comes back, not even the color of his eyes.

Love Lock

I try to make you understand,
My words breathless,
I even use my hands,
But it is a puzzle, a mystery to you.

Summer evenings nuzzle into
A soft green blur and we see
We cannot go on at a crossroad
Holy to one and not the other
For there would be no dedication
Between us, only heaven's blank
Blue.

After a decade of love a shadow
Passed through me until I trembled,
Remembered the words that must
Be said.

I do not love you anymore.
It beats like a soft leather drum.

You say I am hysterical, like all women
Who turn fifty,
You cannot live without me.
It would be a brutal act.

I am a child, estranged to
The gifts meant to engage me for life.

Prize

After a night of lovemaking
I pretended to remain asleep
Butterflies flew out of my stomach
They were all over the room
Floating
Imagining my ecstasy
Fanning air into my fever

He flicked the ash of his cigarette
Stared at the ceiling fan
Other dawns of stern repose

He dressed solemnly
As if for a funeral
Then the doorknob— a slow click

I once won a fifth ribbon
For a watercolor of a bride
Faceless behind a veil
I wonder what number I am now
As butterflies press into the wall

Moon Phobia

I owned the moon
as I cut a large white circle,
scribbled on it and glued it
onto black star-studded paper.

My mother said to clean up
the clutter and since it was
a living room against a universe,
I reluctantly scraped the tools
into my pencil box.

At night in my pale grey room
with sheer blue curtains, I
was afraid to look at the white
thing. Extinguished, on the verge
of spinning to the floor, I hid
under my bed for fear of another
eclipse like a blinking giant eye.

Later, I met a girl with brunette hair
who loved astronomy, could hold
planets in her palm, blow on them
to do her bidding.
Suspecting, she asked me to
admire the galaxy. I quickly
glanced up, said a prayer.
The next year, I married her
yanked open the curtains
and stared the moon down.

Vietnam Sun

I can barely hear you,
But then you
Take long journeys,
Send back erratic postcards
Hinting home soon . . .

My despair you distained
As intimate words and
Midsummer's fierce burning
Of truth trailing our lost passions.

I am patient now. Your love thwarts
My growth, yet I have the fortitude
To withstand your quivering distances

And like a soothing psalm, I wear my
Graduation dress until you do not come home
And it turns dirty yellow like the Vietnam Sun.
In its box now, lace arms in prayer.

Deer Head

Her Way with It

Sitting on a white sparkling
rock in the woods, faraway
I can hear the ocean waves
massage my mind.

There is a woman swimming
into the blue gray furls, mindful
as the sky darkens she must
return to the shore,
and on a blanket wait for her lover's
face to move in and out of the stars.

I have never seen the ocean
and delight in her way with it.
Unafraid, it cannot control her destiny.

On the hot rock, I pretend
my life is not drowning
as long as the woman swims.

Guardianship

They set their white plastic chairs
In a circle, all eyes on the night sky
Between whispers of wind
Glistening pine cones drop on their laps
At night they try to find their faces in
Constellations or an angel looking down
But the enshrouded foggy sky will not lift
One night the fog peels back and
Ecstasy fades the family's demise
Mosquitoes whine and it is chill
But they will not go in
They talk of its glory and future guardianship
For days despite little food
They are sure the viewing will bring good luck
For they are connected to the earth
Just by looking up

The Scarecrow

The crows must leave!
I told my Dad
and he went out
to cut two sticks
and measure his old pants.

I kept behind
and watched him build a man
who had patience, time to endure
a seedling's growth.
We sang two songs
and went into the house.

Five days passed;
the crows fed well.
Several feathered
the hay-speared hat
until Dad rushed out
to punch the pillowed breast
while I cried and held my head.

Murmuring my name twice
and quiet now, quietly now
he took down the self-built man
and sat it on the step.

Questioning it for days,
my head cushioned in its nest,
I heard no answers,
until a fear rose
and I flew away.

English 101

He stood reading a book
In front of students slumped,
Anguished or asleep in his English 101
Class of American fiction meant to
Awaken in them a rare inner life—
Help them find a spouse or stories
For a frightened child carried to bed
His dark tweed coat sleeves
Were smeared with chalk as he read, still saw
The one raised fist of a girl wanting to know
The meaning of life
This would show his imminent failure
For what could he answer?
Origami notes flew through
The air and after class he would
Pick them up, unfold several that
Gave him a moustache or horns
In that pale green room
With high windows, where he wanted
To jump through and fall upon
Dandelions' soft receiving earth
He was as hardened as they were
Only the girl with her fiery need to claim
Hope and knowledge from that desperate
Room would be the one he failed
When he moved her to a higher level
He did not know why she took her breaks
By his door and laughed with a boy named
Alfred who could barely read, yet even
With his dialect rendered a kind of nobility
He felt, listening to them, the boy reading
Aloud a long novel in the blue-green pasture
Outside his classroom, holding their story
High to block the sun. But it was not his

Mary Shellmic

Mary Shellmic wore
a braid to her skirt's hem
and smelled of ash and chicken feed.
She was nineteen
and believed in witch doctors
and a wine cure.
Mary had me thinking of Laughing Water
and copying Pocahontas for stick dolls.
She'd push me the highest
in the crate swing,
and she had a guitar
and sang funny ballads.
From clam shells she made me a necklace
and bracelets of woven hay stems.

I told her at dusk once
on the door step
that she was a lady.
She tore some violets from the ground
and swore
and laughed.

Sleeping Beauty

Inside regal gowns, women
Glide toward mindless love,
Poignant thoughts, recorded unions
The thrown bouquet drops on my shoe,
Startles me, my lace its ribbon.
Earlier, I slid a saffron gown
Over my face, neck, and arms;
Felt the breath of now—
Of the day when confetti would explode
Above the tents and the car,
A wrapped package would drive away.
Later, I walk to my house with its one candle,
Look up at the vulture-laced trees
For someone to lift me over dread
To lay me down in a bed of leaves.

Canvas

If after tragedy—
You name it
If after pain saws within you
And sorrow becomes a microscopic grey
It is enough to allow you again
To be brushed by the tip of a corn moth's
Wings, weaving you dizzy in the goldenrod—
Now telling of fall's long shadow walk toward you,
Of cold's first drifting chill,
Of the pumpkins' awkward spheres
Sliding off ramps for full inspection
Of personality—then
It may be you are now alive,
In a different way,
A way you found because you *were* lost
Inside the realms of unreachable perfection—
It was supposed to happen
In my time,
In my life,
In my way,
But an explosion ripped like a birth
Through the back of your canvas:
A fall scene of a picnic in Gettysburg—
Smoky with its ghosts,
Napkins flying like dainty kites,
Marbled yellow leaves falling
Into children's hair.
Now you know pain will never
Be the same as hard black artillery,
Sleek in the distant sun,
Keeps you on guard.

Yellow Corsage

White tablecloths flutter in the wind
Like sails amidst the chill of Monet blue greens
And guests limp with wine lean toward shoulders
For secrets they have loved and want to hear over.
Having quenched, bled, and torn all that seemed
The harbors of the blessed, women teeter in gowns
Of coal black sequin sparks. They gild the dusk
In a sculptural sway, hoarding wishes as in breeze
Brings a scarf to their lips and holds them there.
No, no one was in the salmon plaster hall
Doting on bad art or what trill was in the air.
Only you with your dark past, burned at the edge,
Smoking in a serpentine form against the pillar,
A girl's yellow corsage hanging shriveled from its pin
In your mind where you touch the pulse, engrave the lines
Of memory being the happiest in the saddest of times.

Deer Head

In the woods of our youth
there was a tree strung
with an antlered deer head.
We played beneath its hollow gaze,
threw nuts at its gaping mouth—
fog seeping from its nostrils,
its fur burnt by ten winters.

Now we cannot find the tree,
let alone our tracks;
yet we yearn
for that gaunt, near-human watch
that set us free from evil—
we being on the ground
and it up there, once
whacked with sticks
that thing which stared.

Emily Rose

Emily Rose was the best one to take over and keep the shop's cold
White manikins properly layered for spring. She bit her lip and
Never giggled, always at work in the folds of satin and taffeta. Her
Mother collected violets in her apron and told her each one was a
Memory, and that you never knew when you'd need all
Of them the most.

She'd allow the girls out to the black balustrade at lunch. Now
Courageous above the town, they would lean in and link arms,
Their sandals half-laced.
Men threw up curses or petals, but eventually all dispersed.

Her childhood was blank. She could take anyone's album and
Say it was hers. If she had a wedding day, she wanted no cake
In honor of the starving. The church bell might ring different
songs.
She was not particular, only in handling
Lace, fringe and velvet so dark she could fall into them.

Once on a breathless spring day she was forced to breathe in.
There was one lover whose laughter startled her, then a butterfly
Flew and landed like a folding pin on the shoulder of her dress.
She wanted it there forever and wanted the lover to go.

Editorial

Hugging a black sweater
A white ribbon tied under her sun hat
The ocean hissed at her, foamed like meringue
Yet she only drew near enough
For her toes to get wet

It could not have her
She heard its huge whisper
Yet stood still and stared
She read of a woman drowning with two children
On a far rock jumping but the blue fury
Was calm then forceful
They just disappeared

Now they are still on the rock
She often comes back, it's alive to her
Newspapers make mistakes
They are still there

Lemonade

I continue my embroidery
Of a butterfly upon lace-leaf greens
Simple enough to sew blind,
Then in nerves you ask
Will I 'bury' you and we laugh.

You tap your frosted glass,
Waiting for my years to entwine
Yours like small, yellow
Roses trapped through a fence.

But, aloneness is a treasure.
That can feign affection,
Unwrap the in and out weave
Of love's uneven stitchery,
Of eyes that see roses bouncing
Yes, no, in the breeze.

I sip the lemonade,
It is cruel I know,
That money plays a part
And roses turn to rot.
Embroidery has a fierce needle,
To calm any emotion down,
And I can do it blind.

Poor Reader

I have never been to the ocean,
But have seen the elegant
Lines of pirate ships
Gliding across the horizon
As if ghosts blew them asunder.

Following each line as a student
Reads in jagged breaths,
A liquid sun pours upon my book.
I lose my place, stand bare foot
Along the shore's pleading ripples
And its soft molds upon the sand.
My name called, I skip toward
The tarnished gold of the sun and sea,
Again, the ships have come, sinister and black
Like the chalk board at her back.

Graduation Dance

She drew the sketch of the graduation dress
In her diary, for it recorded a beginning, a story
Revealed in a glass shoe years ago
How long can images last, the prince in a ballet pose
The ugly sisters and mother harboring evil
False promises, all of it, and yet the dream continues
Up and down the long curving steps to a wretched life
Made more unbearable by the dream
And how many times does she wake up, draws in charcoal
The depths of the band and faceless balloons, the ruby red
Punch bowl she will not go near, the apple she will not bite
The date in a slightly wrinkled suit forgot the corsage
Knowing ahead there would be no first lesson after midnight
With the artist of the yearbook, for God's sake
At her door, she pecks his cheek and a part of her world
Collides with something greater he missed
A story will begin again in roses then a hiss

Attachment

I imagine my grandparents
On top of a tall sunflower, sipping mustard tea,
And calling down: *child, do not climb up,*
For soon we will dry and our seeds scatter.
Starched up to their collars, they always knelt
Inside trunks for memories to attach to a string,
A word to a ball, or some such thing to revive
A story. I sensed their brittle attachment to me,
Drawing their fingers like the sun's rays down my spine.
Tucked in bed I shivered.

Kingdom Come

You do not know what you will know tomorrow.
A king could arrive and ask for your silver for his meal.
The splendor of a pheasant might leave gold dust in the yard;
Or an old man appears asking for water, a word. In matters
Otherwise seen, hallucinations will become liquid
Dreams and shake your life into color, or into a trickle
Of water you once followed to an ancient kingdom--
Waiting your return with a crown, strange scents, a father.
Far cries may foretell a gentle and timely death.
Stories of your own holiness continue only if taking your life
Makes a good legend, otherwise you are an uncurious man.

The Black Empire

Glaucoma windows, a pot belly stove
With skin of ash, a chair with a plastic seat
Fallen on its side, perhaps had flung an old man after stroke.
We crept over boards, hunch-backed and steely
Through cobweb veils of sainthood where
We drew up our knuckled sticks to tear them down. It was
A black empire with half-wit doubts whether to crumble or display
Its dank table another day. We swore to holy secrecy.
After malicious winds buckled it in, each of us kept
A board and nail.

Now my friend's eyes travel architectural print. I drink.
At our usual bar, I talk of the fallen house, watch his cuff links
Reflect chandeliers' jingling tiny bits of sun.
The mirror behind the stalwart bottles shows his contempt
For past losses.
I smoke and nod, see the grey timber's trembling crosses.

Marriage Duel

The day of the duel
our backs touched
for the last time –
our bodies stood
as one shadowed bough
inside sun-prismed trees.

The crystal earth
of moss, tiger lily,
gave way as we paced over holes,
caverned deep in the decay of ice.

Sleepwalkers—our faces gray
in beads of mist,
I turned,
my hand outstretched,
holding, as if in gift,
a tiger lily,
its stem green, almost wholesome
with forgiveness.

Pirate Ship Ring

Washing dishes, I took my wedding ring off
And passed through the mist of a pirate ship
For gold layered in hand towels, braiding
My hair with silks and spices being mixed
With a butter knife, I dropped a frying pan
And awoke to rot, greed, perversions and loose boards
From a crew more animal than man, tattoos rising from skin

I emptied the sink water, slid my wedding ring back on
It was plain to see, my reality split from one dingy
World back into creaking farmhouse boards
From the sparkling ring of sanity's ritual, I see
Black maples tipping westward threaten to rip away
I in my housecoat and ill-dressed for drama
Walking the plank or making dinner

Name

I have long sought my name.
It must have been something unforgettable.
In my attainment I only hear a formless echo.
So I could be a queen or a mermaid lifting her
Fin like a shelled arm.
At birth a name may be a misbegotten fortune
Or a pinnacle of worth to which one aspires.
If I am called I will not know it, thus where
Shall I arrive and claim my personhood?
Perhaps it is a freedom to be unlinked, associations
Dissipated and left to the mind's free roam.
But, who am I? Who will know my travels
Were on the Great Western Plains or in the
Stars of a small boy's telescope? If I chose
A name it might not suit a course in history
And if I lost my way, I might not be called back.
A dream could speak it, but I cannot sleep
Deep enough to hear, for many other names arrive
And bring me nightmare.

The Women by the Creek

At night when the zinnias eclipse
and the crickets
tick like miniature clocks
beneath the moon,
I hear the women
washing their long hair by the creek.

As if shouldering small harps
their fingers deweb each strand.
I watch them –
meditative in this art --
until the dark lace ferns reappear
and I crawl back
from the dew-speared trees,
to your side.

You sleep but do not leave me,
whereas, awake, I journey
into deafer regions
where the creek's shimmering arm
strangles or embraces:
depending on its mood.

Through the Oval

Oak Leaves

When my son left home for the last time,
Oak leaves rolled and scraped
After him as he walked to his car.
I glanced at the old airplane sputtering
Above our heads, circling back, perhaps
As my son did to land and depart the skies'
Mesh of dark, signs of all to fall apart.

For a moment,
Standing tall in his dark, pinstripe suit,
I could not think of where he had to go.
His old kaleidoscope on the seat could make
Designs disappear forever, as bright colors
Spun when once on a hospital cot he held my hand
And I cried for something lost.

On tip toes I held him tight, due to the spinning
Of the day, and when he left, the wind
Shifted and oak leaves gathered in a circle
At my feet, in browns and golds
Like a multicolored wreath.

Pill Box Hat

In fifth grade around lunch, I was drawing
a horse's mane in brown and white pastels,
when a chilling voice on the intercom announced
the President was assassinated. Knowing
I could not go back and unreel this frightening
knowledge, I could not understand why
the teacher picked my pastel as the best and hung
it up in the hall to remind the class, stunned
by the white ribbon that now represented death.
I walked one mile home, passed windows,
all with televisions inside, all knowing
our lives would never be the same.
Home, my mother was weeping, although
I got a slap if I ever did. Father had always
realized what the world should now know: Depend
on no one to take the little emotion you have left.
Having a snack on the living room floor,
I witnessed Oswald's distortion from a bullet.
With the pink pill box hat gone, she looked
like the place all of us were in. The shock
of disbelief, the armor and glamour
taken from those of us who had little in our lives,
but would like to walk into the White House
and see the family there.

Indian Luck

I was proud of Native American Indian in my blood
It meant I was wind, snow, hidden places
Where earth's secrets made longings I could not name
Sad and speechless, shame felt as a yank at my collar—
Another language is in my bent head

Death thoughts kept me alive as burial grounds of
Clam shells poured volcanic energy
Out and up like a cone,
Sliding down like little saucers.

Those who really knew me are now dead,
Yet not dead (I know this for sure)
For I hear the soft patting of their heels
Always sneaking around the chicken shed
Or swinging in the tire wood swing

With me on their lap, wearing gingham
Gripping me for journeys when our souls were
Cut into paper hearts of intricate designs
Unfold when we had to part reaching
For each other's souls as we moved backwards
A stirring sadness in our eyes
Colorless at twilight
Swirling blood in my tiny body,
First touches by my mother who could not cry
For work ahead

Still the never ending love begins,
The forever pain, tears dripping in an empty bowl
My life experiences filling it up with clam shells
Until I bring small spoons of soup
To her lips, blankets soft around her neck,
Love so brittle,

I lift her narrow shoulders up away from the cold earth.
This did not happen, yet I mourned it
As a period of mistaken life no love should have killed.
Indian luck, I was wrapped in wildflowers anyway.

Through the Oval

It is twilight. My hair is damp.
Before a mirror I remember
an aunt's prophesy.
Her words to my mother: Do not worry sister,
someday she will be a real dish.
From our loveless world mother sneered.
Days passed in a chair between cool fans
in that summer of eyelet slips.

A child in an iron mask,
I wept for beauty,
the beast in me sleeping
many years.

I still see
before long closet mirrors
my candled figure attired in wrath,
burning behind a disguise,
evolving in mascara clouds
of powder and rouge in the glass.

And when I forgave,
only a transparency was left.
This I touched and grew old.
I had spun away a childhood
for a face of gold.

Promise

I promised you my soul, thinking that
it was a milky luminous ball I could
throw into the grandness of space.
A tangible spirit, it would return.
But it is like a kite crazy at the string, or an old
woman, pressing hand to heart, when death dissolved
her beloved, now in mist she cannot touch.
If a soul cannot be seen, perhaps it is like faith;
in the end, if forgiven, it will dissolve back into place.
Or my soul promised might travel back as a meteorite,
and hit me with its impact, hard and grey.

Sunshine

After the hospital and intense therapy,
it was a long way back to life's routine stresses.

Home near the creek, I found sanctuary
looking down, hearing lilting familiar sounds.
Marble reflections of water swirled over
brown, lichen pebbles.
The sky cracked open into split fish clouds.

At night I fell asleep with a comforting array
of books, papers, and art objects on the bed.
Three a.m., incessant barking awoke me.
Afraid of dogs since childhood, I gripped
your letter until it was wrinkled.
Having always lived with fear, I trembled
opening the letter and read your lovely lines.

You did not know of the therapy nor the
Indian women who caringly sang
"You Are My Sunshine" before each procedure.

Mt. Katahdin

From my porch in Maine, I can see the mountain
With its lacey snow and jagged teeth sit hard. I do not
Know why it has implicated me in its life,
For I am a plain woman
Some days the mountain is pink, meaning I can
Touch it. It is palatial and sings. I am soaked with fever.
Perhaps newness like a clean, folded wash
Or a dress worn bare will unhinge oak doors bolting its night
Peaks out; just a rock, it adorns me.

Lineage

I would not have told you
If you were going to shudder
Look wounded again at the name given you

A lineage gives you a box of relics
Old eyeglasses, ribbons, a piece of silk
And whirling voices all trying to speak

In drenching rain their tears let you know
Your sorrows were like theirs
In every pattern of a rainbow's floating veins
They said someone had your soft grey eyes

Or even was your twin, sailing in a boat
Her garden hat trailing in the water
Disliking all her eligible men
Wearing a tarnished bracelet
Glinting your names in the sun
Hoping you too found no one

Cross above the Stove

Pray as if you meant it.
Then before we marry I will
Hang the cross above the kitchen stove,
Open the book to parables as if freshly read.

I do not know how to live any other way.
The other ways have vanquished sun and moon,
Stars fall off the cardboard black.

At midnight, I remember my life as a long series
Of cryptic notes I could not understand.
Still it is good to murmur them, prove
My faith is obedient and not just an ornament
Collecting grease through enraptured years--
Testing my cooking of visions and stars
The cross wiped down each spring, as its features
Soften and disappear.

Old Gloves

A family or a gnarled bouquet
over the plates,
reflecting on their namesake.
They brood in bowed praise—
better days better days.

Gothic in the picture window
they sit and I am asked to freeze
these figures behind this eye—

Now as the wind shifts
memory is lean,
I feel dismembered
like a man whose touch is disengaged—
his hands like old gloves
lying in the summer shade.

Meditation

It all comes back.
Memories trudging to and fro
Looking for a place to rest like old men

Who are cryptic, bent, and hold wisdom inside.
At last it matters what shape the clouds make,
Human or divine and why the phantasmal blue

Moves him to think of all the sacrifices,
Selfish or sublime, he has made
Before the mosaic roof caved in.

Despite the piercing clarity of first love when
He also saw his carcass of poverty in its surreal
Wrap of fog, he swung his arms for clearance.

Empowered, he thought, to see all things dead
As alive in whatever shape dreams formed.
Even the near inaudible thud of an apple falling from a tree,

Bruised a mute brown and yellow skin was akin to his
Destiny to drift across the blinding glare of deserts,
And draw his fingers in the sand.

All this came to him as he watched her in the mirror
From the back of her robe-draped chair, the decisive
Motion of her brush through almond strands,

Saying in the grave disenchantment of all reflections,
She could go or stay.

Apple Pie

I iron wanting it to melt the cloth
Church is just a gulp I grip
With dice in my hands

You shouldn't demand a kid to kill

In his Sunday suit sliding down the stair
Rail I wanted to cry from childhood joy
I don't want to cry anymore for I will swell
The river
Put him in a canoe and shove it away
Forever
He always liked to pull the stem off an apple
Now he pulls something off a hand grenade

He liked poetry, brunettes, and snow

Do you think these will save him?
Hell no, my child is changed forever
He is now with friends picked off
Like leaves in the wind
Until as limbs they are gently laid together
Wrapped in blankets of odd comfort

And I am in fatigues running through rubble
With an apple pie

Brownie Camera

I came from the land of soft blue green pines
And did not return, until I thought you had forgotten me.
A child with a Brownie camera snapping suffering
Images best forgotten and undeveloped.

In a world of white falling dogwood petals,
I could forget you, beauty an anesthetic.

I was fond of rented rooms with broken porches,
No dates or names were scrawled beneath the photos
I studied every night.

I took pictures of each tenant, blighted by life, then moved on.
They all wanted a piece of my soul for memory's sake,

Until the camera broke and returning home, I saw stains
On the wall where my pictures had been.

Red Sandals

I am a spinster
And have quietly performed
My life around suspicion, awe,
And pity.

Every day has a charm
I see unhidden by another presence.
The vague perfume of the universe,
The moon pin amidst the cloudy dress,

Red sandals, a necklace tangled for
Decades inside the incense of cedar,
Prepare me for the artlessness of a
Venture toward what I am not.

I have not a hint of visible yearning.
During breezy ocean days, thin blinds
Flap against the boards. Destiny tells
Me in those taps, I can sit quietly and
Wait out my life for a transformation
Gods tangle up.

Or I can drift to the scallop edges
Of the ocean and say hello to a man
Who daily walks by with no expectation I might
Arrive in the red sandals, a knotted necklace
And need--? I do not know. Either way,
It's awfully late for drowning.

Lincoln Memorial

I own a green blanket woven by a traveling weaver
Five years before the Civil War's spread of weeping.
Now the blanket seems invisible for how could something
Exist before the suffering that still lies waste my brain?
The wool's itch, one letter with sketches of how to return
Home, and the final phrases thrown in the air like hats,
Leave me to love the whisper of the life I have.

I would like to stand bridal by the white marble near
Lincoln's memorial.
The steps are an ascent into dreams made from now pale anguish.
It is hard to imagine a whole war in one palm, speeches
Still dripping from his pen whose words I memorize
During windy nights trees swing in agreement.

Beautiful Fur Coats

The door is closed to the oldest friends I have known
And learned to love through absence
Women with beautiful fur coats surround me
 I cannot link arms, must bear cheek kisses
After events where small talk is paramount

Alone with no love and no grief for parents
Who rearranged my bold silk flowers, gave me change
As they traveled through rivulets of alcohol while
I saw life through the windows of cars men drive

In the end, I do not wish to speak to my oldest friends
And tell them what they meant to me, there are embossed
Cards for that and the only real dreams appear when
I close my eyes, try it and you will see

At the Exhibition

The woman walks toward the watercolor.
She mounts the roan horse. Resolute and poised
In the cool aromatic rain after great heat, self-consciousness
Murmurs: Avert. Retract. She cannot
Turn the face of her stiffening will.

In her charcoal riding clothes, no one saw this as her
First dream, as a resemblance to the actual when
Washes of those visionary jumps began to move.

The brumal grey paper and ink-mottled threads
Press dots of rain at her back.
Her eyes conquer the dimensions ahead.

When all have looked, when all in a dark cloud move
On to the next watercolor, she reabsorbs her dignity
When told to step back.

Crosswords

In the gray metal of a hospital,
Sitting upright and holding
My black patent leather purse
I wait to see my mother

It is time to say a few oblique
Words, but I cannot fathom
What they would be
Bawling is out of the question

She spit at the earth with gin
Cigs and crossword puzzles
On her crossed knee, she never
Liked to be interrupted by kids

One day perhaps a puzzle will
Print the exact words of our
Relationship
Then she might see the crosses

Of all its sorrows, and the silences
With missing letters
My black linen suit wrinkled
The nurse says I can go in now

My mother and I look at one another
As oddities, strangers, and freaks
A few words exchanged, I quickly
Hand her the precious crossword

She says she is not up for it and
Falls asleep (perhaps faking)
Then eyes closed asks if I would
Stay awhile as she naps

When she is breathing heavy, I leave
For all letters of our wordless life can
Never work; still she said there wasn't
A crossword hard enough she couldn't do

Symbols

After the memorial, I realized
I had never really known my mother-in-law,
although symbols of her life dangled from
her cumbrous silver charm bracelet.

I could not wear this personal piece,
locked it away for her essence was enough
to carry a lifetime.

In memory, I close my eyes, see beyond
her face our friendship could have been a charm,
but there is no symbol.

Our respect grew as we realized we both were
caring women, calm in our roles handing
the baby back and forth.

Yet, I was afraid, during a quiet moment I might
mention the first words of my baneful childhood
and never stop talking ....

Harp

I am never one person, yet
Am trusted to be, still as wind,
Crouching in hills far away,
To arrive, change into dresses,
And be a childish woman
Clutching a bald doll,
Or a baby in silks to writhe
In a cradle of dirt
You have dug so many times.

Oh day, oh I see it, standing
On that hill, the wind will string
Through the harp of my soul,
And I will turn,

Into a pearl-drained raindrop,
Shimmering and shivering,
Until my cry,
Like a child's wail in wind,
Turns your face toward me.

Deliverance

I knew what I was.

Not a spider stringing
Hieroglyphics in threads perspired by dew.
Not a thin woman, hands folded
Like a bird one upon the other.
Heaviness growing, my body was entombed.

Still, I hear grackles rasp through gauze clouds
At a speed my small hands can stop.
In shawl-chill rooms I write letters of awkward kindness
To loved ones I will never meet.

One day, a slim sheathe, would I forgive
And walk into the arms of men who once stung me
With their crude alphabet, and say farewell
To the woman who knew the constancy of birds?

Scar

I am too tired to lift my hand
And hide the scar on my left cheek
It will blend in with the scrawling
Café title where I am alone
Away from a window
That will be my mirror, my mask

Or I will read a book from the right
Toward the left beneath cotton candy
Lights dulling the line's harsh length

Home a collie gently breathing
On my left side-- he knows
People dare not gaze but squint
Pity and wonder about "The Story"

I told a man I loved
Snow melting on that cheek
His fingers gently drawing its line
I thought we were so close
We would die within seconds
Of one another
And the pity of it is we did

Getting Out

I left home with a small suitcase.
White devours what living there
Never could. I plough through
A vast skirt of snow, holding the suitcase
Over my head until I see the road, cars
Going places I want to go.

I was expected to keep things alive. The fire peach-red.
The table set. The Bibles scattered like black cards;
But the repetition, the scrutiny, thickened my shield
In time a snowy owl at last returned to a branch;
Cast his face in the blurred blue glisten—
Hooted: go, forgiven.

Last Act

Slipping through a Life

The walk-in closet has its say of early dates
Gone awry with a tiny brown silk, its column
Shrivels upon the floor to reveal the transparencies
Of violet, white veins on hands reaching for
After dinner drinks, crackers with olive placed hats

You later sit wilted upon wrinkled sheets,
Unalarmed your thin straps keep falling down
As others notice your homely bones, a ladder to
Your pony tail, a halo to no form and the mirror's
Cosmetic laugh: they soon will never see you
Sip steam from spoons, smear cotton candy
Clouds across the plate of a full moon

At your job a large woman rips hangers from
Dresses as they clack in a heap upon the floor
She then seeks help from you--
You drape her figure in a no nonsense way
Smoothing and shaping, show her the cloth of a smart gray

She envies your long limbs like a tree about to blossom
Near death you slip through your engagement ring
Wearing white muslin

The Cuckoo Bird

Oh, my heart
Oh, my heart

My world view is a colorful, variegated quilt over my lap.
A friend will sew a new skirt for me.
I see who I am, but prefer the woman I was years ago.

I liked to walk down the road, despite speeding cars forcing me
Into the ditch.
Girls would meet once a week and swap stories of our boring lives.
Regretfully, I should have spoken up more for now I am
forgotten.
Character and wit I did not have.

Always reserved, early shame prevented me from living joyfully.
In stillness, I wait for the whistling calls of the cuckoo bird.
Sometimes he does not come, but this is rare.
I hobble to my bedroom window to find the moon. It is company,
something to watch over me.

As long as the cuckoo bird returns, I endure in its afterglow,
knowing this is not the end.

Work Horses

Work horses with hardness drummed
Into their aching heads haul the rolling logs
To the sawdust scoured and scrolled mill

Still harnessed tight, they return home
Like a married wooden pair
Back to the barn where bats
In early evening
Give an acrobatic
Show of wings in salute

I bring them oats
To embrace their ancient pain
I, too, learned with undone chores
Caving in the house, my parents were brittle
Jumped when the phone rang, answered

To the distant caller in the bore and bone
Of holy pastures we will never own

Languages

On her angelic, sharply-angled body I tighten
A quilt over the bones I am afraid to touch, to move
Back into a tender place before their shatter

Rests on the floor, arranged in a language only the
Grave, groping trunks of elephants might know.
Cancer took her piece by piece, her moaning intact
In another consciousness where pain becomes
A child's cry so low—

Our wall, scrolled by quilts of Native Indian design,
Was the space we said they rolled their bodies,
Close to the cheek of the other.
Spellbound, dreams of serene nectar upon their lips,
It was a trick of nature to turn and see life like this.

I will carry her outside and hope the canoe
Will be her last place, the sky an old-fashioned
Mint blue, someone's blind design, after all this,
I question whose.

The Hesper and the Luther Little

I see my father ironing his suit

After high school in early evenings
Kids in scrappy cars park toward
The town's main street and watch other cars
Some dangle their arms on linen-scented shoulders

Our lungs like ovens, we smoke
For freedom is immortality's thrill
Although mothers still make beds

I walk down to the bridge over
The Sheepscot River and pull up the collar
Of my dad's jacket, feel his submerging loss
As I watch two black and ancient coal ships
Sinking together, their rust
And clanging masts crying to be saved

Few in my class graduated and knew
Of no future world beyond town they could aspire
I held my small diploma, but couldn't leave my father
Even when the ships were gone
And there was no place to go

Cigar

I see people sitting on benches
In the park, staring ahead
Hands and ankles folded,
In an aura of quiet sorrow

How do they make life work
For them they wonder?
How will they avoid loneliness?
Find albums askew on the floor
The ache in the throat when the sun
Sets and you no longer feel the pins
In your body urging you to live

They begin to eat crackers
Hold up paperbacks
To pretend reading,
Self-conscious, their arms ache
Then someone looks their way
And sitting beside them on the bench,
Lights up a cigar and instead
Of small talk, shoulders hang loosely,

He speaks slowly: *all this will be gone*
One day, all the benches and wind-cupped
Leaves, in fifty years all we thought here
Will be a silent alphabet

Someone pointed out a zipping blue bird,
He said, "That's what I mean."

Starfish

My father is in a turquoise boat.
The mist holds his ghost back
As the boat is cradle rocked
By hands anxious for it to stop.
The cliffs' black crags are a silhouette
Against the sharp mauves of a
Sky filled with tangled ribbons.
His fishing line stings the water
And radiates the ethereal ripple
Of something lost, over and over again.
Now eighty, he has cheated death, outrun
The bravest and could pluck from his friends'
Grave last wishes, words he now cannot utter.
Before a sun-gilded light house, he remembers
A rebirth, when as a boy, he jumped
The moss-glazed rocks, then flung himself
Like a starfish upon the sand.
Noon, the sun is like a sword pinching his head.
When he finally yanks a vase-shaped bass into the boat,
For the first time, its speckled and textured iridescence
Transfixes and troubles him.
He feels the ghost flop twice,
Enter his body.

Sorrow

It's delicate. The story of my life.
I always hear it crashing
Like a large oak upon the wildflowers.
The sun laughs and I seek alcoves of maple.
Figuring it out is impossible when your
Soul vents its pale fog over a worn bridge.
Each decade forgets the other.
There is a sorrow without a name.
It tortures my history.

On the operating table, I am about
To fall into false sleep,
Yet, I am happy to crush that sorrow
For one second into eternal white.

Days of Rage

The indigo blue bird comes and goes,
but I have yet to see it.
Will it be a sign of inexpressible beauty
to come or a sign of aging?
I look in the mirror, sagging neck, wrinkles
and feel I have lost my youth but for my eyes.

I am another person now, staring too long
at the designs of my teacup, jumbled by life.
I imagine the warmth of a collie against my legs,
lilacs in every room, someone calling my nickname.

Repudiating loneliness, I empty drawers,
smash dishes, overturn lamps until exhausted.
Pounding the counter, I yearn for a voice.

A dash of blue flickers past the window.
It does not matter now.

Two Men on a Bench in a Great City

I am no more
Than I am in this moment;
And yet, I am everything I have been.

It's a wonder, isn't it?
Our generation signals us to
To carry on, yet we are the last to know.
The grandchildren will tangle our lives:
You'll be in the wrong story,
And I will be left out.

I have unearthed the secret. It is kinder
Than I thought and the gargoyles above
My head lap the rain, rust sealed at their lids.

What did you say?
Oh, I have come to that too.
Finality. We can breathe now.
Dreams had their way with us
And those lost we tossed out.
No one was to blame. No.

Anything left is a reverence
I keep for my mother.

Out of the Country

In the move much was minimized,
I felt no loss or memory of my hands
Around linen, crystal, or a silver tea set.

Outdoors the clothesline ropes
Tied to the wide expanse of the sycamores,
I remember billowing sheets flowing into
My face draping my body.

From the hill, the creek in front of
The farmhouse below glinted
Green and brown reflections,
Sometimes a piece of sky and cloud
Rippled like a heavenly skirt.

I sat down in the grass and watched
A car turn the corner at the creek and house,
A loss filled me.

Now in a small apartment
With a meager patio I no longer
Own beauty and buttercup spreads.
I wake, tidy up, and go to bed
Where dreams, suffice to say,
Are now my wild travel,
Life so quiet during the day.

The Gas Station

A father never speaks, but stares into a lifetime
Of years when his town friends were alive
Always talking at the gas station about the fish
The deer, the sons of disappointment
Now he is the only one left and often
Hears his name called as if at the gas station
They still lounged around its corners
Drinking and smoking and eating their wives'
Heavy dumplings may have taken some early
But, he would like to lasso them all back
Visit the verdure of their Sherwood Forest
Some forgot about it in the end, how their arrows
Speared like needles through hard leather
No one special came to mind for their thoughts
Were a dough of kinship after fermented cider
Oh, one did not smoke, but whittled dolls for kids
He had none nor a wife nor a dog, just land he
Walked around and around until the sunset
He said it was his ceremony of prayer
Everyone laughed, a little uneasy knowing
He had pancreatic cancer and no one to tidy
His room, then one day he went somewhere
Grim hollowness lasted a month, maybe more, real funny
Mentioning all this slowly to his wife
After pea soup and a lit pipe, he noticed
She still huffed and puffed with jealousy
Mad she was not there to sweep the shavings
Knock the drunkest off his stool so she could
Laugh, relax like a fool

Duties

Now there is another thing I have to do.
Die. Just when the heavy green drapes
Need to be taken to the *Peter Pan* cleaners
And the fridge I have to crawl in needs cleaning

That cardinal is still flying into the window
Until its feathers blink bright red on the sill

I will have to call my closest and only friend
First, for I tell her everything and I will have
To be there for her to the dead end

Then I will have to shop and fill the freezer
For at least a month and get the *Merry Maids*
To come in here for my husband
Three beer cases will get him over the initial
Shock for he has a lot of buddies at Huber's Hub

I am going to check into a hotel and put my
Feet up, write in my journal then bawl my head
Off just when I remember I wanted to give my
Dresses and jewelry to my sister

My son in Iraq will be a trooper
He has seen and heard everything
I am telling him nothing
That pecking cardinal bugged him too

A Little Life

When she died a broad chalk
Cracked the sky and thunder
Shivered billows of smoke

They knew the sequestered
Ways she darted through life
Always with a hanky or with alarm
Pressing logs against the door

She never had a secret chat
Or dressed a table with napkins
Meaningless remarks made her brood
And sometimes she peered to see in the mirror
Any sanity to pool her eyes

Such a little life consumed by rage
One night jagged sobs ignited the town
They heard just another woman's
Rant and rave storm after storm

Wooden men, daughters running through
The spaces of stars for these wooden men
To lift warm spoons to their lips

Last Act

I did not want to grow this old.
More questions than answers.
The big one like the moving colors
Of a garnet is abstract, yet yearns
For my lost attention to its
Black- blood brilliance resetting.

I tap my cane upon stone,
Hoping it will pierce then tarnish
The lament of my generation, mad
With gossip, our hats pinned to our hair
Never to be loosened by wild wear.

It startles me to now desire passion,
Now when life, a ritual of bowl, soap, and bed,
Sees the clarity of love
Become the magic of real things:
Dusk before a velvet-antlered dark,
Jagged rows of rocks you want to
Follow to a clot of daisies at the end.

What truth to see the wrinkling and
Fanning of the butterflies
In painted colors dance, then breathe
And mock my frequent and awed search
For the rippled swirling of my skirt
Brought to the lips, click, click!

I do not know how to prepare for death.
Local eyes say: *see her now, then you won't.*
Somewhere as night comes on like a slipper pat, patting,
I am now alone on a patio, sipping rum and coke,
Thinking this a proper ending, or a beginning
As when I first jumped into flour-sifted snow.

117

About the Author

Judith Ann Levison was born into a logger's family and raised on coastal Maine. At fifteen she was published in *The New Yorker*. Inspired by her poetry, a high school teacher assisted and guided her toward higher education. She holds degrees from Mount Holyoke College, Hollins University, and Drexel University.

Her poems have appeared in numerous journals and she has published two chapbooks, *Oak Leaves* and *Sand Cradle*.

She currently lives in Pennsylvania with her husband where she pursues her poetry career and paints abstract watercolors.

www.ingramcontent.com/pod-product-compliance
Lightning Source LLC
Chambersburg PA
CBHW030945090426
42737CB00007B/541